I'm Reading About

ILLINOIS

The Prairie State!

GALLOPADE

by Carole Marsh

Printed and Manufactured in Peachtree City, GA., USA
www.gallopade.com

Book design: John Hanson

Editorial manager: Janice Baker

Illinois is a great state.

It is one of a kind.

What makes Illinois special?

Let's read about it

and see!

NATIVE AMERICANS

Who lived in Illinois first?

Native Americans did!

They moved around to find food.
They hunted in Illinois' woods.
They fished in Illinois' rivers.
They gathered fruits and seeds and nuts.

EXPLORERS

The first explorers came to Illinois in 1673.
They came from the country of France.

Jacques Marquette and Louis Joliet
were their leaders.
They were looking for new land!

SETTLEMENT

Men came from France to America.
They started the first settlement in Illinois.
They named it Cahokia.

Cahokia was built along the
Mississippi River.

Cahokia
Cahokia

STATEHOOD

Illinois was the 21st state to join the United States of America!

Isn't it great,
to be a state!
I bet Illinois
could hardly wait!

Illinois became a state in 1818.

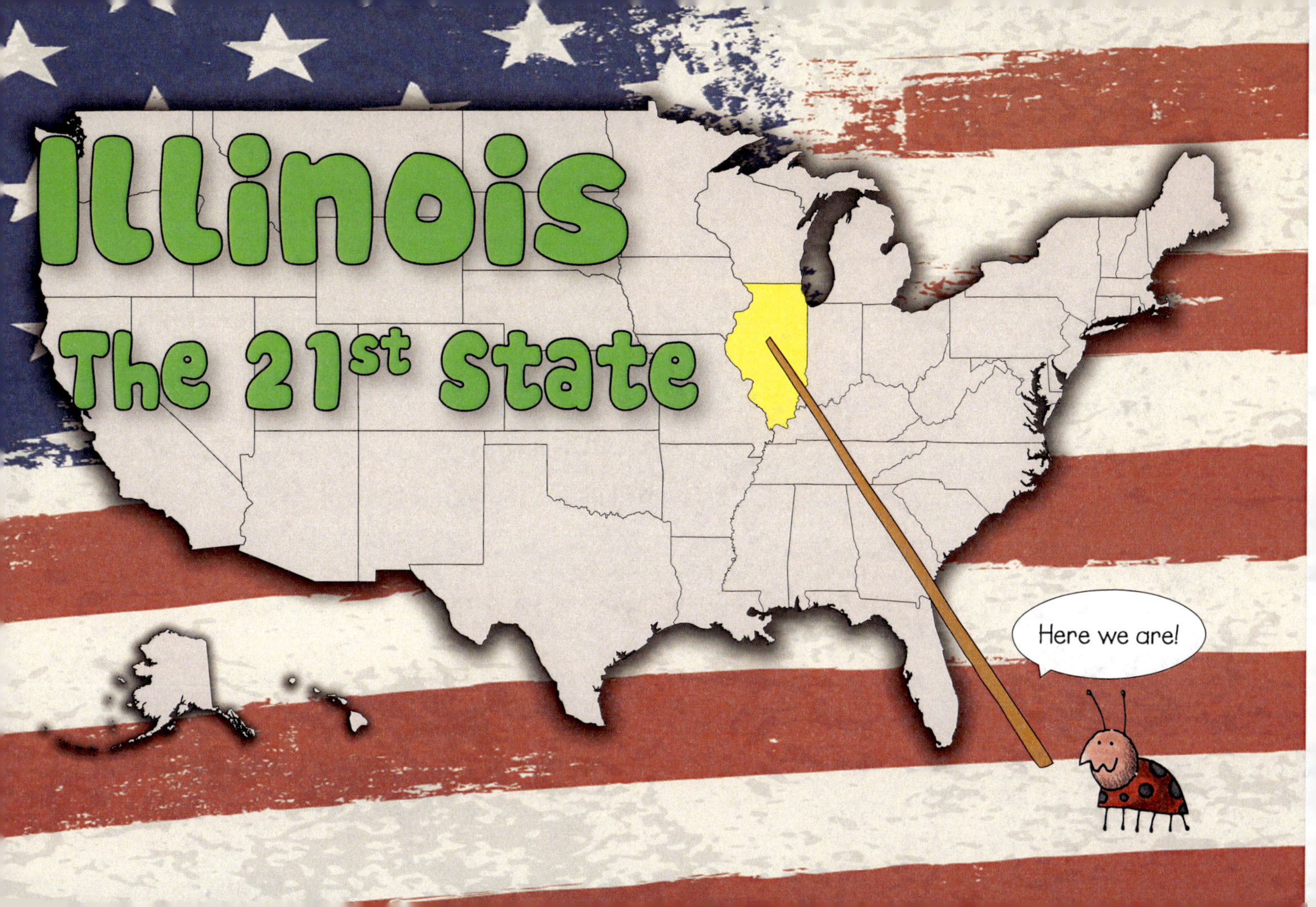
Illinois
The 21st State
Here we are!

FLAG

I am the state flag.
I was adopted in 1970.

What color am I?
I am white.

Look at me.
What else do you see?

I fly high over the state of Illinois!

UNION
NATIONAL
SOVEREIGNTY
STATE
1868
1818
ILLINOIS

CAPITAL

Say hello to Springfield,
the capital city of Illinois!

There is an important building in Springfield.
It is the State Capitol.
Illinois laws are made there!

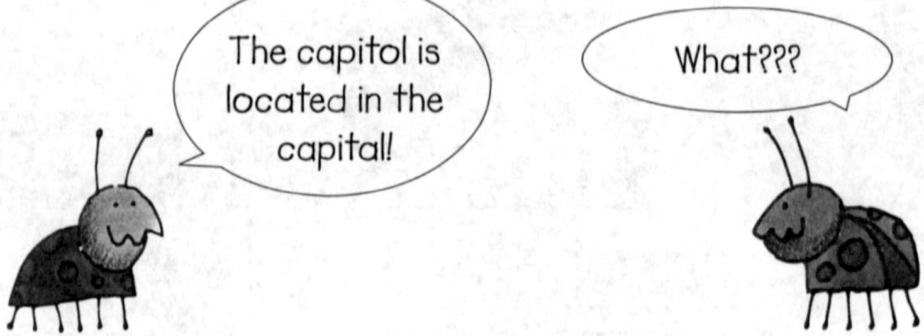

Capitol

SEAL

I am a seal,
but I am not the State Seal.
If I were, I would be very important.
I would be stamped on many official papers.
(Ouch, that might hurt!)

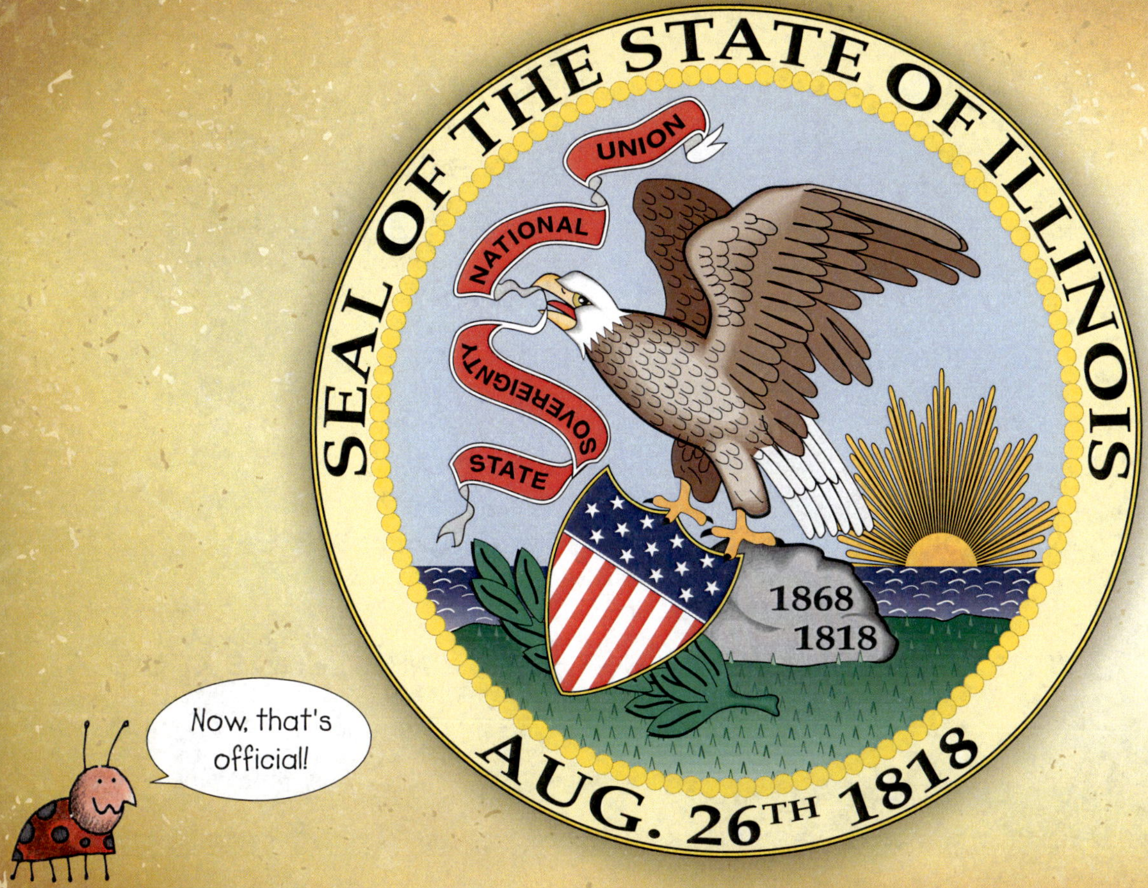
SEAL OF THE STATE OF ILLINOIS
UNION
NATIONAL
SOVEREIGNTY
STATE
1868
1818
AUG. 26TH 1818
Now, that's official!

NICKNAME

State nicknames are fun!
State nicknames are great!
They share fun facts
about each state!

Illinois' nickname is "The Prairie State."

Most of Illinois was once covered with prairie grass!

The Prairie State

BORDERS

Look at Illinois.
Illinois is in a region called "the Midwest."

Illinois borders five other states.
Find them on the map!

Illinois comes from a Native American word that means "warriors."

Borders

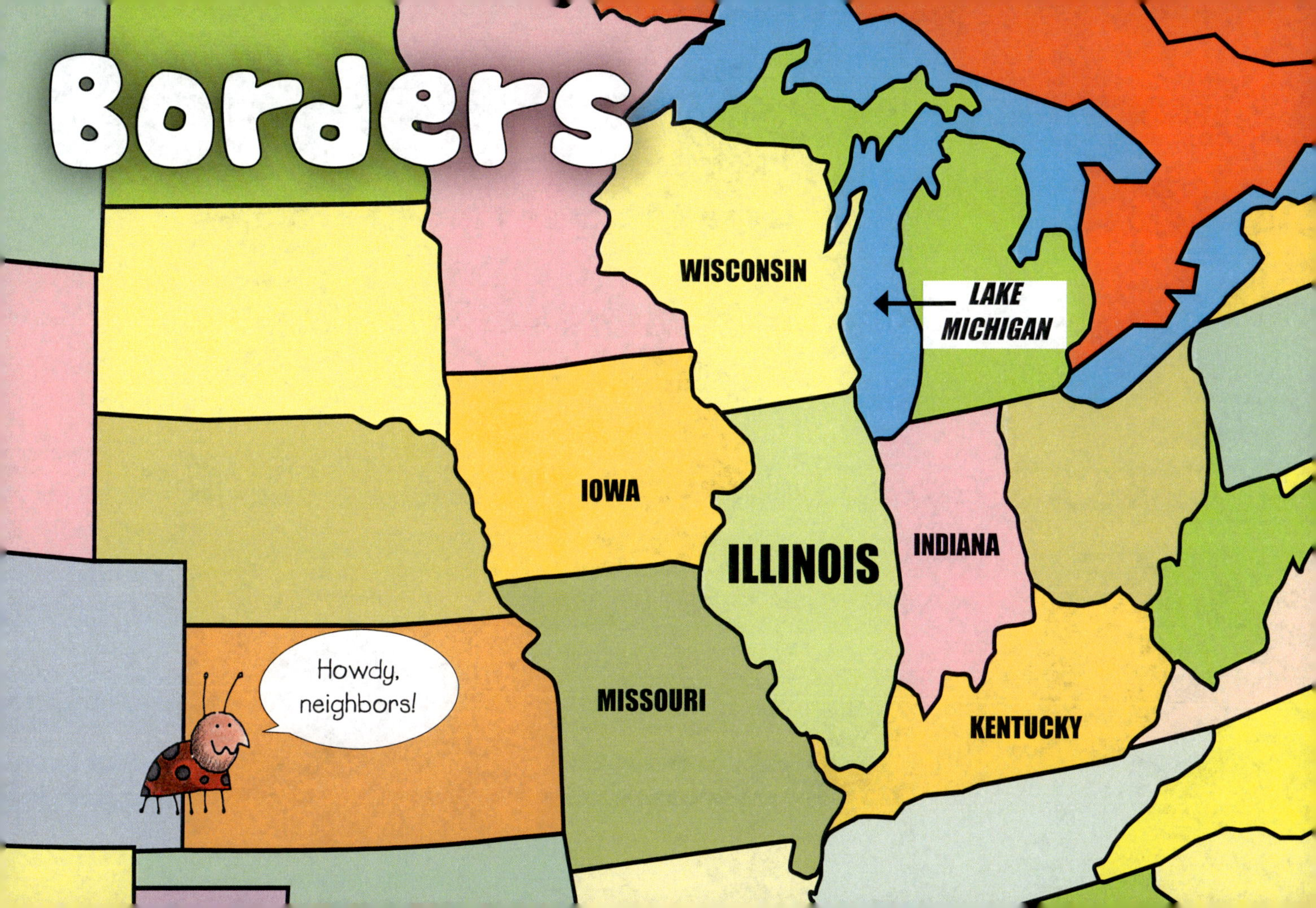
WISCONSIN
LAKE MICHIGAN
IOWA
ILLINOIS
INDIANA
MISSOURI
KENTUCKY
Howdy, neighbors!

PRESIDENT

The President is the leader of our country.
He lives in Washington, D.C.
That is the capital of the United States.

The President lives in a big house
called the White House.

Several United States presidents are from Illinois!

Abraham Lincoln
16th President
Ulysses S. Grant
18th President
Ronald Reagan
40th President
Barack Obama
44th President

Many famous people

Black Hawk
Sauk Indian Chief

Walt Disney
Creator of Mickey Mouse, Disneyland, and Walt Disney World

Hillary Clinton
First Lady, U.S. Senator, and U.S. Secretary of State

call our state home!

Oprah Winfrey
Television talk show host

Mae Jemison
First African American female astronaut

Michelle Obama
First Lady and wife of President Barack Obama

PEOPLE

Cardinal

BIRD

I am the state bird, and I fly
over Illinois, proud and high.

As I fly, up in the sky,
I flap my wings to tell you "Hi!"

The Illinois state bird is the Cardinal.

Violet

FLOWER

I am the Violet.
I am the state flower.

I grow where it's warm and sunny.
I bloom in spring and summer.
I help make Illinois beautiful!

Look at me! Smell me!
I have dark purple petals!

White Oak

TREE

I am a White Oak—I'm the state tree.
All over Illinois is where to find me.

My roots run deep, they keep me strong.
I can live for hundreds of years—that's very long.

I stand up straight, big and tall.
Don't climb too high—it would hurt to fall!

Monarch Butterfly

I am the Monarch Butterfly
I am the state insect.

I flit and I fly from flower to flower.
I am looking for nectar to drink.

Look at my beautiful wings.
What colors do you see?

Lake Michigan

Let's go to the lake!

We can wade in the water.
We can ride on a boat.

We can jump off the dock
onto an inner tube float!

Lake Michigan, Illinois' Great Lake,
is home to many animals:

Fish Snakes Birds Turtles Salamanders and More!

Prairies

PRAIRIE

Illinois was once covered in prairie land.
The tall golden grass
swayed in the breeze.

The prairie is flat.
There are no trees.
It stretches as far as the
eye can see!

Rivers

RIVERS

There are many rivers in Illinois.
The Mississippi River forms the western border of the state.

The river habitat is home to many animals:

Birds **Deer** **Snakes** **Frogs** **Fish** **and More!**

The first explorers to Illinois traveled down the Illinois and Mississippi Rivers!

Willis Tower

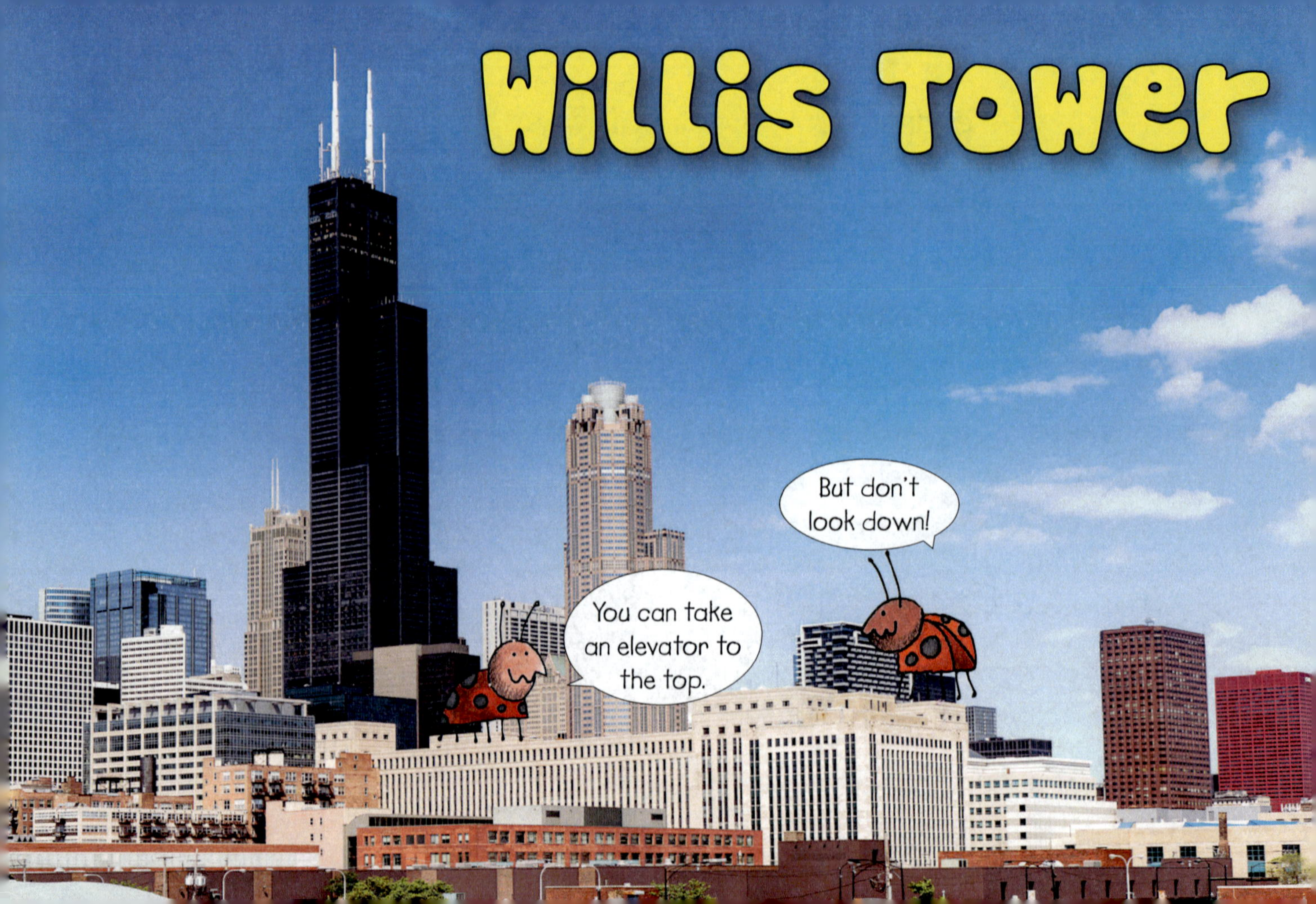

LANDMARK

The Willis Tower is a skyscraper.
It used to be called the Sears Tower.
It is the second-tallest building in the United States.
It is 108 stories high!

Many people visit the Willis Tower in Chicago every year. They can see all of Chicago from the observation deck!

Illinois Crops

AGRICULTURE

Illinois has many farms.
Why?
Because Illinois has good soil and a mild climate!

Some of the top crops grown in Illinois are:

Corn **Soybeans** **Hay** **Wheat**

Sports in Illinois

SPORTS

Baseball! Basketball! Football!
Illinois has it all.

Whether you like to watch or play,
You are sure to have a ball!

Bears **Bulls** **Cubs**

White Sox

Fighting Illini

& More!

Illinois: Land of Lincoln

Illinois is called the "Land of Lincoln."

Abraham Lincoln moved to Illinois
when he was 21 years old.
He lived in Springfield until he became President.

Abraham Lincoln was one of
the tallest U.S. Presidents!

GLOSSARY

astronaut: a person trained to travel in a spacecraft

climate: weather conditions in an area over a long period of time

elect: to choose someone by voting

habitat: a place where plants or animals naturally live

laws: rules made by the government

nectar: a sweet liquid produced by plants, especially flowers

observation deck: a high platform where people can look down at the area around them

region: an area that has similar characteristics

settlement: the first community in an area

skyscraper: a very tall building with many stories